W9-AKT-686

IN FOCUS

THE #METOO MOVEMENT

by Marty Erickson

BrightPoint Press

San Diego, CA

BrightP◇int Press

© 2020 BrightPoint Press
an imprint of ReferencePoint Press, Inc.
Printed in the United States

For more information, contact:
BrightPoint Press
PO Box 27779
San Diego, CA 92198
www.BrightPointPress.com

ALL RIGHTS RESERVED.
No part of this work covered by the copyright hereon may be reproduced or used in any form or
by any means—graphic, electronic, or mechanical, including photocopying, recording, taping,
web distribution, or information storage retrieval systems—without the written permission of
the publisher.

LIBRARY OF CONGRESS CATALOGING-IN-PUBLICATION DATA

Names: Erickson, Marty, author.
Title: The #MeToo movement / Marty Erickson.
Description: San Diego, CA : ReferencePoint Press, [2020] | Series: In focus
  | Includes bibliographical references and index.
Identifiers: LCCN 2019003315 (print) | LCCN 2019005004 (ebook) | ISBN
  9781682827185 (ebook) | ISBN 9781682827178 (hardcover)
Subjects: LCSH: Rape victims--Juvenile literature. | Sexual abuse
  victims--Juvenile literature. | Sexual harassment--Juvenile literature. |
  Sex crimes--Juvenile literature.
Classification: LCC HV6558 (ebook) | LCC HV6558 .E75 2020 (print) | DDC
  362.883--dc23
LC record available at https://lccn.loc.gov/2019003315

CONTENTS

TIMELINE

2006
Activist Tarana Burke founds Just Be Inc. and starts the "Me Too" movement.

November 29, 2017
News anchor Matt Lauer is fired from *The Today Show* for sexual misconduct.

October 2017
The *New York Times* publishes a story about film producer Harvey Weinstein. Several women accuse Weinstein of sexual assault. Weinstein is fired from his film company. Actress Alyssa Milano creates the MeToo hashtag on Twitter.

2006

2017

January 21, 2017
The Women's March happens in Washington, DC.

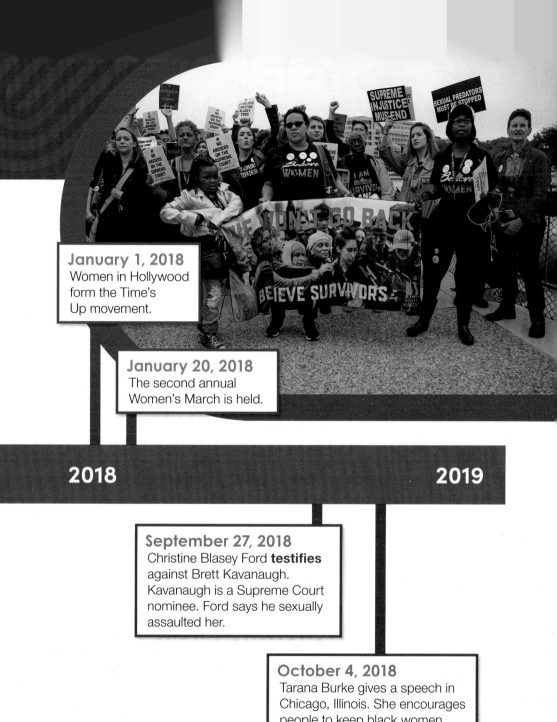

January 1, 2018
Women in Hollywood
form the Time's
Up movement.

January 20, 2018
The second annual
Women's March is held.

2018   **2019**

September 27, 2018
Christine Blasey Ford **testifies**
against Brett Kavanaugh.
Kavanaugh is a Supreme Court
nominee. Ford says he sexually
assaulted her.

October 4, 2018
Tarana Burke gives a speech in
Chicago, Illinois. She encourages
people to keep black women
and girls at the center of the
#MeToo movement.

STARTING A MOVEMENT

In October 2017, actress Alyssa Milano posted on Twitter. She invited survivors of sexual assault or harassment to write the words "me too." Millions of people responded. They shared their experiences. Some talked about how they had been harassed. Others shared stories of rape. "Me too" turned into a hashtag.

In 2018, actress Alyssa Milano shared her own story of sexual assault.

Hashtags are used on social media. They collect posts from different people. Users can search hashtags to find all the posts about a subject.

The phrase "me too" was already being used. Milano did not know this. Tarana Burke had first used the phrase years earlier. Burke is an African American activist. In 1997, she was a youth counselor at a camp. A girl shared her story of sexual abuse with Burke. Burke did not know how to help the girl at the time. She wanted to say, "Me too." But she was not ready to tell her own story. Burke's "Me Too" movement came out of that encounter. She founded Just Be Inc. in 2006. Just Be Inc. empowers girls of color. It gives girls a safe space to talk about sexual assault.

Activist Tarana Burke gives speeches around the country to raise awareness of sexual assault.

THE POWER OF "ME TOO"

Burke says the phrase "me too" is powerful.

This is because it has many meanings. She

explained its meanings in a 2017 interview.

She said, "It's a bold declarative statement

that 'I'm not ashamed.' . . . It's [also] a

statement from survivor to survivor that

The "me too" hashtag inspired protests across the country.

says, 'I see you . . . I understand you and I'm here for you.'"[1]

Twitter users gave Burke credit for creating the phrase. For Burke and many activists, the movement is more than just a hashtag. It is about raising awareness.

#MeToo quickly moved to other social media sites such as Facebook. Today, conversations about sexual harassment and assault are becoming more public. Harassment is when someone purposefully makes another person feel uncomfortable. Assault is when someone attacks another person. The #MeToo movement is making more people aware of these issues. Many survivors have come forward. Several people accused of these crimes are facing consequences for the first time. Activists are hopeful that lasting change is coming.

CHAPTER ONE

WHAT IS THE #METOO MOVEMENT?

On October 5, 2017, the *New York Times* published an article about Harvey Weinstein. Weinstein was a film producer. Many women accused him of sexual misconduct. Weinstein denied their claims. But more women soon came forward with their own stories.

Police escort Harvey Weinstein (middle) out of court after a hearing in June 2018. Weinstein pled not guilty to rape and sexual assault charges.

Weinstein had used his power to take advantage of women. Many survivors had stayed silent for years. They had been afraid to share their stories. They thought Weinstein would ruin their careers.

Weinstein was fired from his film company. He had been a member of many production committees and organizations. They took away his memberships. Harvard University took back an award it had given him.

TOXIC MASCULINITY

Toxic masculinity is a phrase used to describe a narrow definition of manhood. Boys are pressured to fit gender **stereotypes.** They are taught that they need to act a certain way in order to be manly. Violence is one trait that society considers manly. So is a high sex drive. Sex drive is a person's desire for sex. These messages are everywhere. They are toxic. They create harmful behaviors. Changing these behaviors is challenging.

Actress Rose McGowan claimed that Weinstein raped her. McGowan became a leader in the #MeToo movement.

#MeToo started on Twitter soon after the Weinstein story broke. Within a year, more than 140 other high-powered people were accused of sexual misconduct. The survivors who shared their stories included

Celebrities such as actress Whoopi Goldberg (third from left) joined in marches for women's rights inspired by #MeToo.

actresses and professional athletes. The

#MeToo movement gave them the courage

to speak up.

#MeToo is a social movement. Social

movements arise when there is an injustice.

People want to change something about

society. Social media helped expand the

#MeToo movement's influence. Leaders organized #MeToo rallies and protests. These events happened around the world.

EMPOWERING SURVIVORS

Sexual assault survivors may feel ashamed or guilty. They may blame themselves for the assault. One survivor said, "I assumed it was my fault. . . . I always smiled and said hello to my boss. I think he must have thought I was flirting with him."[2] Many survivors do not share their stories for these reasons.

The #MeToo movement gives survivors a voice. Millions of people have shared this hashtag. They created a global community. #MeToo has changed how people talk about sexual assault. But there is also a lot of pain within the #MeToo community. It is difficult for people to share

SELF-CARE

Some sexual assault survivors have a hard time reading #MeToo stories. It makes them relive their experiences. Self-care can help survivors cope. Self-care is a series of actions people can take. It involves checking in with themselves and asking, "Am I okay?" This helps people identify what makes them uncomfortable. Then they can take steps to relieve that discomfort. Therapy helps many survivors. Limiting time spent on social media can also help. Then survivors may be less exposed to assault stories.

and read stories of sexual assault. Some survivors felt pressured to share their stories. Not everyone was ready to come forward. Some people may never be able to speak up publicly. Seeing so many posts brought up painful memories. There were few ways to prevent #MeToo posts from showing up on people's social media feeds.

A TIPPING POINT

#MeToo sparked conversations about gender. Many sexual assault survivors are women. In most societies, men have more power than women. This creates inequality. One issue is the gender pay gap.

Women are often paid less than men. In the United States, women earn about 80 cents for each dollar that a man earns.

Many women are harassed or assaulted in the workplace. The Equal Employment Opportunity Commission (EEOC) released a study in 2016. It found that as many as 85 percent of women face harassment at work. Sexual harassment is a type of discrimination. Discrimination is illegal.

Some companies punish women for speaking out about harassment. The abuser is usually a man in a higher-level position. In some cases, a man may

A woman protests for better pay in Toronto, Canada. Many countries around the world have a gender pay gap.

not promote a woman if she denies his

advances. Then the woman does not

get a higher-paying job. Women who

experience workplace harassment may quit

their jobs. Some have to start over again

at lower-paying jobs. Harassment and assault can increase the gender pay gap in these ways.

Many activists have called #MeToo a tipping point. A tipping point is a moment when important changes occur. Activists think the movement will change how survivors are treated. They think it will hold more abusers **accountable**.

VICTIM BLAMING

Abusers often do not face consequences. In many cases, people do not take survivors seriously. They may even blame the survivors. This is called victim blaming.

Many #MeToo activists bring attention to both sexual violence and broader women's rights issues.

People make excuses for the abuser. They

may say the woman was wearing too little

clothing. Or they may say her clothing

was too tight. They think her appearance

invited the abuse. They do not examine the

abuser's behavior.

In September 2018, Christine Blasey

Ford testified against Brett Kavanaugh.

Kavanaugh was a nominee for the

US Supreme Court. President Donald

Trump had nominated him. Supreme Court

REPEATING HISTORY

Ford was not the first woman to accuse a
Supreme Court nominee of sexual misconduct.
Anita Hill testified against nominee Clarence
Thomas in 1991. Hill had worked with Thomas.
She made several claims. She said Thomas
had made sexual comments toward her.
Still, senators confirmed Thomas to the
Supreme Court.

justices decide on important court cases. Their rulings have a wide influence. Ford accused Kavanaugh of sexual assault. She said the assault happened when they were teenagers. She described the assault before the Senate Judiciary Committee. This committee confirms Supreme Court nominees. Senators questioned Ford during her testimony. Some blamed her for the assault. Others thought she was making it up.

Two other women also accused Kavanaugh of sexual misconduct. They said he had been drunk. Ford said Kavanaugh had been drunk when he assaulted her too.

Many senators did not see Kavanaugh's past drinking problems as an issue. Ford answered all their questions. Kavanaugh did not. He avoided answering some questions. Still, the committee voted to confirm his appointment to the Supreme Court.

GENDER EQUALITY

Many steps toward gender equality were made in 2018. More women ran for political office in the United States than ever before. Many abusers received punishment.

But other events showed there was plenty more work to do. #MeToo is trying to

Women gathered in Washington, DC, to support Christine Blasey Ford during her testimony in 2018.

change how the world talks about sexual

violence. Survivors are coming together.

They are supporting one another. No one

should have to suffer in silence.

CHAPTER TWO

WHO ARE THE #METOO MOVEMENT'S LEADERS?

Celebrities helped the #MeToo movement gain traction. There was a flood of support from women in Hollywood. Many of these women felt a personal connection to the issue. They were survivors. They had been assaulted

Tarana Burke (right) stands with Mira Sorvino (left), an actress and supporter of the #MeToo movement.

or harassed. Some of the women were

actresses. Others were writers or directors.

But they are not the only leaders of the

movement. People from all around the

world support #MeToo.

On January 21, 2017, about 4 million people gathered in Washington, DC. That was Trump's first day in office as US president. The crowd marched near the US Capitol building. The march was a protest against sexual assault. It was also a protest against Trump. Trump had made sexist comments about women. Some women accused him of sexual assault. Speakers at the march talked about their own experiences of assault and harassment. Similar marches were held across the United States. Marches were also held around the world. This event

People protest outside the National Museum of Natural History in Washington, DC, during the 2017 Women's March.

became known as the Women's March.

Another Women's March was held one year

later. About 2 million Americans participated

in the 2018 march.

TIME'S UP

Some activists criticize #MeToo. They say

it only lifts the voices of people in power.

They say **working-class** people are left out. These people may not feel empowered to share their stories. Activists encourage the movement to include all survivors.

VIOLA DAVIS'S SPEECH

Actress Viola Davis spoke at the 2018 Women's March. She said:

I am always introduced as an award-winning actor. But my testimony is one of poverty. My testimony is one of being sexually assaulted and . . . seeing a childhood that was robbed from me. . . . I know that the trauma of those events are still with me today. . . . That's what allows me to listen to the women who are still in silence.

Quoted in Matthew Dessem, "Watch Viola Davis' Stirring Speech at the 2018 Women's March," Slate, January 20, 2018. www.slate.com.

In November 2017, *Time* magazine published a letter. Latina farmworkers wrote the letter. They were part of a group called Alianza Nacional de Campesinas. The women supported survivors in Hollywood who had shared their stories. They wrote: "Even though we work in very different environments, we share a common experience of being preyed upon."[3]

Many people were inspired by this letter. Three hundred women in Hollywood came up with an idea. These women were writers, directors, and actresses. They wanted all survivors to be heard. They started a

Many #MeToo activists also support the Time's Up movement.

movement in January 2018. They called

it Time's Up. #MeToo had started the

conversation. Time's Up was going to be

part of the solution.

Time's Up joined with the National

Women's Law Center. They set up an

online account to raise money. Their initial

goal was to raise $15 million. By late 2018,

they had raised more than $22 million. This

money pays for legal services for survivors.

Survivors have to pay lawyers to bring a

CHANGE IN HOLLYWOOD

Time's Up and #MeToo took center stage at awards ceremonies in 2018. Some people wore white roses at the Grammy Awards. The roses signaled that they supported sexual assault survivors. Guests at the Academy Awards recognized the two movements. Some wore "Time's Up" pins. Some talked about the movements in interviews. Others took a different approach. They purposefully wore clothing designed by women. This gesture showed that they supported gender equality.

lawsuit against their abusers. These fees can be expensive. Many people cannot afford them. The Time's Up **fund** helps survivors afford legal assistance.

INCLUDING WOMEN OF COLOR

Tarana Burke gives talks around the country. She makes sure #MeToo includes women of color. Women of color are more likely to face workplace harassment than their white peers. Burke spoke in Chicago, Illinois, in October 2018. She reminded the crowd that #MeToo was started by black women. She said leaders needed to bring more women of color into the movement.

Many women of color, such as television producer Shonda Rhimes, have become involved in the #MeToo movement.

Burke invited two black women to the stage. One was sixteen-year-old Angelina Cofer. She said, "[#MeToo is] **dominated** by a lot of white women. And it's good that they're sharing their stories. But I would like to see more color in the movement."[4]

Burke also spoke about #MeToo's influence. She said that #MeToo is "a global movement of survivors that . . . centers the people who are pushed to the margins."[5] Activists around the world have started their own movements against sexual assault. Some of these movements began before #MeToo. But #MeToo helped bring widespread attention to the issue.

GLOBAL INFLUENCE

Between October 2017 and October 2018, #MeToo was tweeted more than 19 million

Swedish singer Isa Tengblad speaks at a #MeToo event in Stockholm, Sweden, in 2017.

times. People in 196 countries searched for it on Google. Nearly 30 percent of #MeToo posts were in a language other than English. These facts point to a global influence.

#MeToo has given many survivors a sense of community. This is especially important in places where survivors are

Many #MeToo and women's rights activists are working to empower young girls.

often ignored. India and Middle Eastern countries shame women who speak out about rape. Online platforms give survivors a way to share their stories.

Before #MeToo, many people did not know how common sexual misconduct is. It is widespread in many countries. In a survey of Egyptian women, 99 percent reported that they had experienced sexual harassment. Awareness of the issue is the first step toward change.

CHAPTER THREE

WHY IS THE #METOO MOVEMENT IMPORTANT?

Many women face consequences for speaking out about sexual misconduct. Other movements tried to raise awareness of this issue before #MeToo. But they often did not create lasting change. Many people hope #MeToo will be different.

Women march against sexual violence at a rally in India in 2014.

Rape is common in India. In 2012,

a woman was **gang raped** in India.

She died from her injuries. This incident

caused national outrage. Women in India

led protests in major cities. Politicians promised change. Some of the nation's laws did change. The government set up courts to hear rape cases. It also increased the length of prison sentences for people found guilty of sex crimes. It introduced the death penalty for child rape cases. But these changes did not have much effect. Rape was still widespread. In 2016, about one hundred cases of rape were reported in India each day. Researchers think this number is low. They estimate that 99 percent of female rape survivors do not report their rape. Many people

Schoolchildren protest for better laws against sexual violence in India in 2015.

were frustrated. They had hoped India's

new laws would have more influence.

LESSONS FROM THE MOVEMENT

#MeToo stories show the consequences

that occur when people do not respect

INDIA'S LAWS

In 2017, Human Rights Watch reviewed the changes that had been made to India's sexual violence laws. It published a report. It found that the changes had not made much of a difference. No one enforced the new laws. Police often did not help sexual assault survivors. One woman said she had been raped. The police threatened to imprison her father if she did not drop the charges.

each other's boundaries. These stories could help teach young people about consent. Consent is an agreement to engage in sexual activity. Sexual activity without consent is rape or assault. Many people first enter into romantic relationships as teenagers. It is important for them to understand consent. They can carry this lesson into their relationships.

Adults can also learn important lessons from #MeToo. Young survivors may share their stories with adults that they trust. This includes teachers and parents. It also includes coaches. Adults have to be ready to have these conversations. They should listen to survivors. They should take survivors' stories seriously. They have the power to help survivors.

LARRY NASSAR

In January 2018, Larry Nassar was on trial. Nassar was a doctor who worked for

Activists prepare for a Women's March in Toronto, Canada, in January 2018.

USA Gymnastics. More than 300 women

and girls accused him of sexual abuse.

More than 160 of these women came

forward during the trial. They each had a chance to tell their story.

The case against Nassar began in 2016. It started with one woman. She accused Nassar of sexual abuse in an article that came out in the *Indianapolis Star* newspaper. Soon more women came forward. They shared similar stories. In the 2018 trial, Nassar was found guilty. He was sentenced to 40 to 175 years in prison.

Many gymnasts had filed complaints against Nassar before the trial. Complaints stretched back to 1997. Nassar had worked at Michigan State University. The university claimed it had not mishandled complaints. The US Olympic Committee (USOC) and other organizations began their own investigations. They found that many officials knew about the gymnasts' complaints. But officials had not taken the complaints seriously. They failed to take action. Kerry Perry was among these officials. Perry was president of USA Gymnastics. The USOC forced her to quit. This incident shows how important it is to listen to survivors the first time they come forward. Taking immediate action can help prevent future sexual assault.

USA Olympic gymnasts Simone Biles (middle) and Aly Raisman (right) spoke up about how Larry Nassar had abused them.

STREET HARASSMENT

#MeToo stories have helped people

better understand sexual harassment.

Many people think they have never

experienced sexual harassment. But most

people have experienced it at some point in

their lives. Harassment includes unwanted

comments or touches. These actions are

meant to intimidate or offend someone.

Many people think that because something

is common, it is okay. This is especially

true with catcalling. Catcalling occurs when

someone makes a sexual comment about a

person. This is a type of street harassment.

It happens in public when the person is

passing by. Catcalling is aggressive. People

who are catcalled often feel threatened.

Sexual Harassment

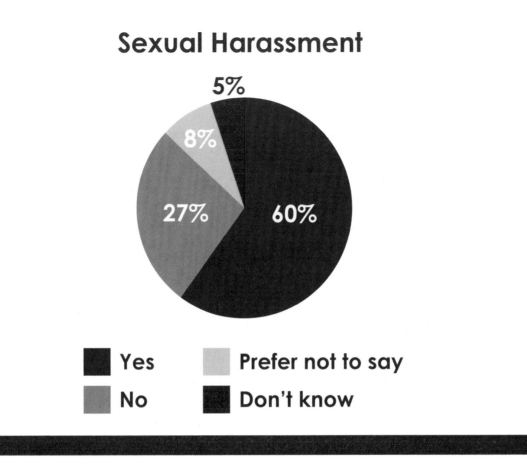

The above graph shows the results of a 2017 poll. The poll asked a group of US women whether they had been sexually harassed.

Street harassment often goes unreported. An article in the *Daily Telegraph* reported, "Those who report street harassment are regularly . . . [shown] as over-reacting."[6] Many people do not take street harassment seriously. But it is a widespread problem. In large cities, women may face street harassment daily. This can affect their schedules or lifestyles. For example, they may avoid walking in certain areas. They may limit the time they spend outside their home. Street harassment restricts their movement and freedom in these ways. #MeToo is shedding light on this problem. #MeToo is also inspiring protests. In New York City and other large cities, women wrote catcalls on sidewalks with chalk. Some were catcalls that had been directed at the women. Others

were catcalls the women had overheard.

This demonstration showed how catcalls

can turn violent. One phrase read, "You

better learn to answer a man when he

speaks to you!"[7]

TERRY CREWS

The #MeToo movement has often centered women's stories. Actor Terry Crews says that is important. But it is also important for male survivors to talk about their experiences. Crews was groped by a male film agent in 2016. But no one believed him. They told him the agent was just playing around. Crews says that men need to hold their male friends accountable. #MeToo helped him tell his story.

Actor Terry Crews shared his story of sexual assault on Twitter in 2017.

#MeToo shows people how widespread sexual misconduct is. It has helped redefine who is affected by sexual misconduct. Men have started sharing their stories too. For a long time, many people believed men could not be victims. But that is not true. The world's definition of sexual misconduct gets a little bigger with each #MeToo story that is shared.

CHAPTER FOUR

WHAT'S NEXT FOR THE #METOO MOVEMENT?

The #MeToo movement does not show signs of slowing down. Many survivors are still coming forward. Activists are seeking justice for them. The movement is not just about continuing the conversation. People also hope #MeToo will create lasting changes.

Women protest at a Million Women Rise march. Million Women Rise is a group in the United Kingdom that works to end violence against women.

PROTESTS

#MeToo started online. It quickly spread to

the streets. The Women's March was one of

many protests against sexual misconduct.

Another large protest occurred in late 2018. On November 1 of that year, Google employees staged a walkout. A walkout is a type of nonviolent protest. More than 20,000 Google employees left their offices. Google has headquarters in several countries. Google employees in California joined these protests. They gathered outside the company's building. They were protesting the company's actions. They said Google had protected sexual abusers. One former employee was paid $90 million to quit after he was accused of sexual harassment. Employees saw

Google's US headquarters is in Mountain View, California.

this as a reward instead of a punishment.

Protesters held signs. One said, "Happy to quit for $90 million. No sexual harassment required."[8]

Leaders of the Google protest gave the company a list of demands. One demand was that Google change its policy for

Many activists are working to hold abusers accountable for their actions.

reporting sexual misconduct. Employees

who made these reports had to give up

their right to **sue**. They could not file a

lawsuit against their abuser. One employee

said, "The first thing that [the company] did

was silence me."[9] She said a coworker had

drugged and attempted to assault her. But she had to keep working with that person.

Sundar Pichai is Google's chief executive officer. He talked with the company's managers about the issues protesters brought up. Google did not make any immediate changes. But protesters hoped changes would come in the future. Pichai said he was committed to making changes.

HELPING ALL SURVIVORS

Celebrities made #MeToo famous. But activists hope the movement will begin to focus again on working-class people. Many people of color are working class.

Women of color face both gender and racial discrimination.

Women of color face a higher rate of sexual violence than other women. This rate is especially high among Native American women. The Centers for Disease Control and Prevention (CDC) did a survey in 2010. The CDC interviewed 148 Native American women in Seattle, Washington. Ninety-four percent said they had been raped.

Working-class people face high rates of poverty and unemployment. They have fewer resources than their wealthier peers. Women of color have less power and influence than white women. Native American women face additional barriers to getting help. Tribal courts decide cases on reservations. These courts cannot punish people who live outside the reservation. In many cases, the abuser does not live on the reservation.

Undocumented immigrants also face more challenges. Many do not report assault or harassment to police. They fear

deportation. They cannot legally be deported in these cases. But many undocumented immigrants do not know this. They do not want to take the risk. #MeToo teaches survivors how to get help.

BYSTANDERS

Leaders hope to create safer communities. One way to do this is by empowering bystanders. Bystanders are people who are around when something happens. They may be present when sexual misconduct takes place. Bystanders can help victims. But most of the time, they do not take action.

THE BYSTANDER EFFECT

Someone who witnesses a crime is less likely to call the police if other people are around. This is called the bystander effect. People believe another bystander will call the police. So they do not take any action. This is dangerous. Victims can be seriously hurt. Bystanders should not rely on others to do the right thing. They should take responsibility.

There are many actions bystanders can take. They could interrupt the situation. This could be as simple as standing between the two people. Or bystanders could invite the victim to do an activity. For example, they could invite the victim to get a cup of coffee. This removes the victim from the situation.

Aisling Chin-Yee (left), Mia Kirshner (middle), and Freya Ravensbergen (right) founded #AfterMeToo in 2018. The group brings attention to sexual misconduct in the workplace.

Sexual harassment may happen in a workplace. Bystanders may know the harasser in these cases. They can confront the harasser. This does not have to be done in the moment. It can happen later, even in an email. The bystander could ask, "Do you realize how your actions affected that person?" This response makes harassers confront their behavior.

Not all bystanders feel safe confronting harassers. Even in these cases, bystanders can offer help. They can ask the victim if she is okay. Many victims blame themselves. Help can come in many forms. It could be as simple as reassuring the victim that she did nothing wrong.

SYSTEMS OF POWER

#MeToo helps people understand systems of power. Systems of power describe who has power in a society. Often a few people have power over many others. Race and class determine who has power. So does gender. In much of the world, white men have the most power. Black women typically have the least power.

Systems of power affect all people. This includes the leaders of the #MeToo movement. Sexual misconduct arises from an abuse of power. Asia Argento was one of the leaders of the #MeToo movement. Argento is an actress and a director. She claimed that Harvey Weinstein had raped her. Then in September 2018, actor Jimmy

Asia Argento has a long and established career in Hollywood as an actress and a director.

Bennett accused Argento of sexual assault.

He said the incident happened when he

was seventeen years old. Argento was

thirty-seven years old at the time. Argento

denied his claims. But other #MeToo

leaders distanced themselves from her.

Activists say this incident should spark

conversations about systems of power.

Tarana Burke posted on Twitter. She wrote

that people should become "comfortable

with the uncomfortable reality that there

is no one way to be a perpetrator . . .

and there is no model survivor."[10] #MeToo

leaders agree that the news about Argento

is unfortunate. They think it could taint

people's opinions of the movement. But

the movement is larger than one person.

SOCIAL MEDIA CAMPAIGNS

Social media is known for short-lived campaigns. People move quickly from one cause to another. Real change is often not possible over social media. Other hashtag campaigns about sexual assault exist. But few are used as often as #MeToo. #MeToo is used as often as #BlackLivesMatter. #BlackLivesMatter brings attention to police violence against African Americans. Several thousand people post #MeToo stories each day. This leads researchers to believe that #MeToo is not just a passing fad.

It includes many activists around the world. They continue to help people understand and address sexual misconduct.

GLOSSARY

accountable

held responsible for one's actions

deportation

the process of sending an immigrant back to their country of origin

dominate

to be the center of attention

fund

a collection of money to be used for expenses

gang rape

rape committed by a group of people

stereotype

a common belief about a group of people that is usually negative and untrue

testify

to make a formal statement under oath in court

working-class

working for low wages, usually in manual labor

SOURCE NOTES

INTRODUCTION: STARTING A MOVEMENT

1. Quoted in Cassandra Santiago and Doug Criss, "An Activist, a Little Girl and the Heartbreaking Origin of 'Me Too,'" *CNN*, October 17, 2017. www.cnn.com.

CHAPTER ONE: WHAT IS THE #METOO MOVEMENT?

2. Quoted in Beverly Engel, "Why Don't Victims of Sexual Harassment Come Forward Sooner?" *Psychology Today*, November 16, 2017. www.psychologytoday.com.

CHAPTER TWO: WHO ARE THE #METOO MOVEMENT'S LEADERS?

3. Quoted in Megan Garber, "Is This the Next Step for the #MeToo Movement?" *Atlantic*, January 2, 2018. www.theatlantic.com.

4. Quoted in Morgan Greene, "#MeToo's Tarana Burke Tells Local Activists Movement 'By Us and for Us' Must Include Women of Color," *Chicago Tribune*, October 11, 2018. www.chicagotribune.com.

5. Quoted in Morgan Greene, "#MeToo's Tarana Burke Tells Local Activists Movement 'By Us and for Us' Must Include Women of Color."

CHAPTER THREE: WHY IS THE #METOO MOVEMENT IMPORTANT?

6. Quoted in Andrea Nagel, "Catcalling Isn't Flirting, It's Sexual Harassment. Here's Why," *Sunday Times*, August 5, 2018. www.timeslive.co.za.

7. Quoted in Gurvinder Gill, "Catcalling: Women Write in Chalk to Stop Street Harassment," *BBC*, July 2, 2018. www.bbc.com.

CHAPTER FOUR: WHAT'S NEXT FOR THE #METOO MOVEMENT?

8. Lauren Hepler and Sam Levin, "'You Can't Erase Us': In Silicon Valley, Google Workers Share Assault Stories," *Guardian*, November 1, 2018. www.theguardian.com.

9. Quoted in Lauren Hepler and Sam Levin, "'You Can't Erase Us': In Silicon Valley, Google Workers Share Assault Stories."

10. Quoted in Arwa Mahdawi, "The Future of #MeToo: 'The Movement Is Bigger Than Asia Argento,'" *Guardian*, September 2, 2018. www.theguardian.com.

FOR FURTHER RESEARCH

BOOKS

Duchess Harris, JD, PhD, with Myra Faye Turner, *Political Resistance in the Current Age*. Minneapolis, MN: Abdo Publishing, 2018.

Heather C. Hudak, *The #MeToo Movement*. New York: Crabtree Publishing, 2019.

Kate Schatz, *Rad American Women A-Z: Rebels, Trailblazers, and Visionaries Who Shaped Our History . . . and Our Future!* San Francisco, CA: City Lights Publishing, 2015.

INTERNET SOURCES

Lauren Camera, "#MeToo Goes to School," *U.S. News & World Report*, January 8, 2018. www.usnews.com.

Wendy Lu, "What #MeToo Means to Teenagers," *New York Times*, April 19, 2018. www.nytimes.com.

"Want to Prevent Harassment and Assault in Schools? Listen to Students," *NEA Today*, November 19, 2018. www.neatoday.org.

WEBSITES

The Joyful Heart Foundation
www.joyfulheartfoundation.org

The Joyful Heart Foundation raises awareness of sexual assault, domestic violence, and child abuse. It educates and empowers survivors.

The National Sexual Violence Resource Center (NSVRC)
www.nsvrc.org

The NSVRC collects and shares research about sexual violence.

Rape, Abuse & Incest National Network (RAINN)
www.rainn.org

RAINN is the largest US anti-sexual violence organization. It offers guidance and a support network. RAINN also operates a hotline for sexual violence survivors.

INDEX

IMAGE CREDITS

Cover: © Sundry Photography/
Shutterstock Images
4: © Sundry Photography/
Shutterstock Images
5: © Rachael Warriner/
Shutterstock Images
7: © Featureflash Photo Agency/
Shutterstock Images
9: © lev radin/Shutterstock Images
10: © lev radin/Shutterstock Images
13: © lev radin/Shutterstock Images
15: © JStone/Shutterstock Images
16: © a katz/Shutterstock Images
21: © Louis.Roth/Shutterstock Images
23: © Shawn Goldberg/
Shutterstock Images
27: © Rachael Warriner/
Shutterstock Images
29: © Kathy Hutchins/
Shutterstock Images
31: © 3000ad/Shutterstock Images
34: © Sundry Photography/
Shutterstock Images
37: © Kathy Hutchins/
Shutterstock Images
39: © Hans Christiansson/
Shutterstock Images
40: © Shawn Goldberg/
Shutterstock Images
43: © arindambanerjee/
Shutterstock Images
45: © arindambanerjee/
Shutterstock Images

48: © Shawn Goldberg/
Shutterstock Images
51: © Leonard Zhukovsky/
Shutterstock Images
53: © Red Line Editorial
56: © Jaguar PS/Shutterstock Images
59: © John Gomez/
Shutterstock Images
61: © Uladzik Kryhin/
Shutterstock Images
62: © Ms Jane Campbell/
Shutterstock Images
64: © Shawn Goldberg/
Shutterstock Images
68: © Shawn Goldberg/
Shutterstock Images
71: © Featureflash Photo Agency/
Shutterstock Images

ABOUT THE AUTHOR

Marty Erickson is a genderqueer writer living in Minnesota. Marty uses the pronouns "they/them/theirs." They write books for young people full time and like to go hiking.